What a Year

written and illustrated by

Tomie dePaola

A 26 FAIRMOUNT AVENUE BOOK

PUFFIN BOOKS

PUFFIN BOOKS
Published by Penguin Group
Penguin Young Readers Group,
345 Hudson Street, New York, New York 10014, U.S.A.
Penguin Books Ltd, 80 Strand, London WC2R ORL, England
Penguin Books Australia Ltd, 250 Camberwell Road, Camberwell, Victoria 3124, Australia
Penguin Books Canada Ltd, 10 Alcorn Avenue, Toronto, Ontario, Canada M4V 3B2
Penguin Books (N.Z.) Ltd, 182-190 Wairau Road, Auckland 10, New Zealand

First published in the United States of America by G. P. Putnam's Sons,
a division of Penguin Putnam Books for Young Readers, 2002
Published by Puffin Books,
a division of Penguin Young Readers Group, 2003

3   5   7   9   10   8   6   4

THE LIBRARY OF CONGRESS HAS CATALOGED THE PUTNAM EDITION AS FOLLOWS:
De Paola, Tomie.
What a year / by Tomie dePaola
p.   cm.—(A 26 Fairmount Avenue book)
1. De Paola, Tomie—Childhood and youth—Juvenile literature.
2. De Paola, Tomie—Homes and haunts—Connecticut—Meriden—Juvenile literature.
3. Authors, American—20th century—Biography—Juvenile literature.
4. Meriden (Conn.)—Social life and customs—Juvenile literature.
5. Meriden (Conn.)—Biography—Juvenile literature.
[1. De Paola, Tomie—Childhood and youth. 2. Authors, American. 3. Illustrators.]
I. Title.   PS3554.E11474 Z4785 2002   813'.54—dc21   [B]   2001019921
ISBN: 0-399-23797-6 (hc)

Puffin Books ISBN 0-14-250158-1

Printed in the United States of America

To all the wonderful friends and neighbors
who lived around us
at 26 Fairmount Avenue.
And you too, Mario.

Chapter One

I was always glad to see my brother Buddy's birthday come and go. It was on August thirty-first, and that meant three good things. We went to the Labor Day family picnic on Mount Tom in Wallingford with all the Downey relatives. It was time to go back to school. And it was MY birthday on September fifteenth.

This year, 1940, was my very first birthday in our new house at 26 Fairmount Avenue. Well, almost new. We had moved in last January, a few days after New Year's.

I was going to be six years old. I was in Miss Kiniry's first grade class. And I was going to have a birthday party at school!

That's because when Mom asked me who I wanted to have at my birthday party, I said, "My whole class."

"Well," Mom said, "that might be hard. Some of the children live in other neighborhoods. Their folks might not have cars to pick them up and bring them here and take them home again. Let me call up Miss Kiniry and see if we can have a party with your birthday cake at school. Would you like that?"

Well, I guess I would.

Miss Kiniry said YES!

But there was a big problem. September fifteenth was on a Sunday. So the question was, would I have my birthday cake in school *before* or *after* my real birthday? Mom and Miss Kiniry decided *before*, on Friday the thirteenth, would be best. "A very nice way to end the week," Miss Kiniry said.

Friday the thirteenth! Well, I'd just have to be careful not to walk under a ladder, let a black cat cross my path, or break a mirror. I didn't want anything to go wrong for my "almost-birthday party."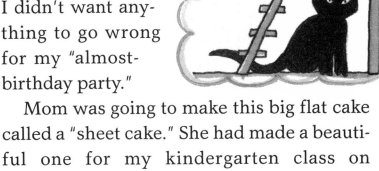

Mom was going to make this big flat cake called a "sheet cake." She had made a beautiful one for my kindergarten class on Valentine's Day.

On the Wednesday before my birthday, Mom met me after school. We went downtown to the big bakery on West Main Street in Meriden. They sold all kinds of decorations for cakes made out of colored sugar

3

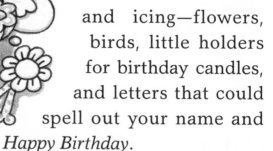

and icing—flowers, birds, little holders for birthday candles, and letters that could spell out your name and *Happy Birthday.*

Mom let me pick out the ones I liked for my sheet cake. They were on paper cards. I picked out white, yellow, and blue ones. I also picked out some little, round, silver sugar balls. They would look very fancy on my cake!

The next day when I got home from school, the cake was out of the oven. It was cooling on the kitchen table, and Mom was mixing the frosting in a bowl.

"Oh, good," she said, "just in time to help decorate your cake. What color do you want for the frosting?" I thought a light green would look nice with the white, blue, and yellow decorations.

"I'll put some lemon juice in it so it will have a nice sweet-and-sour taste."

Mom let me shake the green food coloring

from one of the little bottles in the food-coloring box. I tasted the frosting. It was delicious.

"Can I give Maureen a little taste?" I asked. My baby sister was in her carriage watching.

"Just a teeny bit," Mom said.

I put some frosting on my finger and let Maureen lick it off. She made a funny little face, gurgled, and laughed.

I helped Mom spread the frosting on the cake.

Next, we soaked the paper that the decorations were on in a pan of water for just a few minutes. Then we took the letters and numbers off very carefully and put them on the cake. We spelled out HAPPY 6TH BIRTHDAY, TOMMY. I wanted it to say "TOMIE," but Mom said that was pushing it. The teachers still wouldn't let me spell my name T-O-M-I-E in school.

We put the real date on it, too.

SEPTEMBER 15, 1940.

Then we decorated the cake with all the flowers and birds and the tiny silver balls. Finally we put the sugar candleholders in place—six of them!

I thought it was the most beautiful birthday cake I had *ever* seen. Wait till my class saw it the next afternoon.

Chapter Two

"Happy almost-birthday, wake up," Mom called. I jumped out of bed. I was six years old—well, almost. I dressed and flew downstairs to have breakfast. There at my place was a small pile of almost-birthday presents.

Buddy was already eating. "How about some shredded wheat with hot milk on it?" Mom asked. That was one of my favorites.

Mom took two shredded-wheat biscuits out of the box with Niagara Falls on it and put them in a shallow bowl. She dotted them with butter, sprinkled sugar on top, and poured in the hot milk.

After I finished eating, I opened my presents. There was a kazoo, a bag of glass marbles, and a box of pick-up sticks. "You'll get your real presents on Sunday when we get home from Wallingford," Mom told me. (Every Sunday we went to Wallingford to visit Tom and Nana, my grandfather and grandmother.) "And don't forget, because it's your birthday, you get to do one thing you really want to do." That was a custom in our house. "Have you thought about it yet?" Mom asked.

"I'm still thinking," I said. "I'll tell you when I come home for lunch." (We came home from school for lunch every day.) I had an idea, and I hoped Mom would let me do it.

At school, Miss Kiniry said "Good morning, class" like she always did. "We will have reading this morning instead of this afternoon."

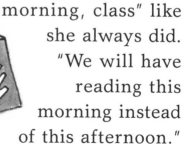

(I bet that was because of my party.) "I'd like the blue group to come up to the front first. The rest of you will please practice your letters until I call your group." She didn't say anything about my birthday. We started our lessons just like a regular morning.

Maybe when we had "Morning Milk" Miss Kiniry would say something. Every morning two of the older kids would come in with a crate full of small bottles of cold milk, regular or chocolate, and put it on the activity table in the front of the room. Miss Kiniry would take out a book and call out the names of the kids who had brought in their dimes for the week and mark off their names. She always called everyone's name. (I found out later that if someone didn't have the money, Miss Kiniry paid it so that everyone would have milk.)

Finally it was time for Morning Milk. One by one we went up to the activity table, took our bottles of milk and straws, and went back to our desks. Then the "Cracker Monitor" went up and down the aisles and put a paper napkin on each of our desks. Next, we each got a couple of crackers. The person chosen to be the Cracker Monitor had to wash their hands very, very carefully.

We all drank our milk and munched our crackers. Now Miss Kiniry would say something. But she didn't. Maybe she forgot that it was my birthday and we were going to have a party in the afternoon. Maybe I should remind her. I whispered to Jack Rule, "I think Miss Kiniry forgot about my birthday cake."

"Tommy, no whispering, please," Miss Kiniry said.

The bell rang for recess. We went out to play. The bell rang to come in. We filed back into class. We did some more work. Finally, the bell rang, and it was time to go home for lunch.

"All right, class, have a nice lunch. Oh, and I have a surprise for you."

Now Miss Kiniry would mention it!

"This afternoon, we are going down to the auditorium to see a movie."

Then Miss Kiniry said it!

"And after the movie we are going to celebrate our classmate Tommy's upcoming birthday with a wonderful cake. See you after lunch."

Miss Kiniry smiled at me as I went out the door. "Happy birthday, Tommy. You were such a good sport. I bet you thought I forgot."

"Oh no," I said, "I knew you were only teasing me."

Chapter Three

When Buddy and I got home for lunch, I could tell by the smell that Mom was making grilled cheese sandwiches. This was terrific. Almost all the things I like to eat the best, all on the same day.

The sheet cake was sitting on the dining room table, covered with waxed paper to protect it. I couldn't wait for my class to see it.

"Okay, boys, sit down and eat your lunch." Mom turned on the radio. There were short fifteen-minute programs at noon, including fifteen minutes of our famous cousin Morton Downey, the Irish tenor, singing. We never missed *that*!

"Oh, Morton, what a beautiful day," a woman's voice said. That was the lady that Cousin Morton chatted with in between songs. He called her just "Lady."

"Yes, Lady," Cousin Morton said. "Guess what? I'm going to dedicate my next song to a little cousin of mine in Connecticut. Sunday will be his sixth birthday. This one's for you, Tomie." And Cousin Morton sang "Wabash Moon" just for me!

I looked over to see if Buddy was jealous. He wasn't. He was too busy eating grilled cheese sandwiches.

"Okay, boys," Mom said. "Time to get back to school. And Tomie, did you decide the one thing you want to do for your birthday?"

"Yes, Mom," I answered. "I want to cook my own dinner. I want to cook a POP-EYE!"

"Okay, Tomie," Mom said. "We'll talk about it when you get home this afternoon.

Now hurry up. I'll see you later at school for your party!"

When we got to school, Miss Kiniry's class joined the other first grade—Miss Delaney's—and the second grades—Miss Gardner's and Miss Fisher's—in the auditorium in the lower part of the school to see the movie.

Miss Kiniry said we were going to see a "silent" movie. When it started, I knew why. There was no sound, no music or anything. It starred a little girl named Baby Peggy. But she didn't sing or dance like Shirley Temple, my favorite movie star. All she did was run around and cry.

Finally, the movie was over. We all lined up and went back to our classrooms. And boy, what a surprise!

While our class was at the movie, Mom and Uncle Charles, my mom's brother, had decorated the classroom with balloons

15

and colored crepe-paper streamers. Miss Kiniry—or somebody—had written "Happy Birthday, Tommy" on the blackboard. On each desk was a little paper basket with gumdrops and jelly beans in it and a "Dixie Cup" filled with ice cream. Under the lid of the paper cup was a circle of waxed paper. You peeled it off, and there was a photo of a movie star. Guess who I got? Ginger Rogers, a lady who tap-danced.

Then Miss Kiniry lowered the window shades, and Uncle Charles told me to close my eyes.

"Okay, Tomie. You can look now!"

I opened my eyes, and there was the cake with six lit candles. Everyone sang "Happy Birthday." I made my wish and blew! All the candles went out!

Then Uncle Charles had a good idea. "Why don't you take a piece of cake down to Miss Burke and Miss Philomena?" Miss Burke was the principal, and Miss Philomena was her secretary.

"Can I give a piece to Mr. Walters, too?" I asked. He was the janitor.

Mom cut three pieces of cake and put them on plates. Miss Luby, the school nurse, wasn't there that day, or I would have taken her a piece, too!

After the party we got to ride home from school in Uncle Charles's car.

"Thanks, Mom, that was great," I said as we went in the door at home.

"Well," Mom said, "how about making a pop-eye tonight, on your almost-birthday? We have to go to Wallingford on Sunday, so we might be getting home kind of late."

So later, when Dad got home, I made a pop-eye for my own dinner! Mom tied an apron around my waist. I took a piece of bread and cut a hole in the middle of it. Then I cracked an egg into a cup. Dad got the small

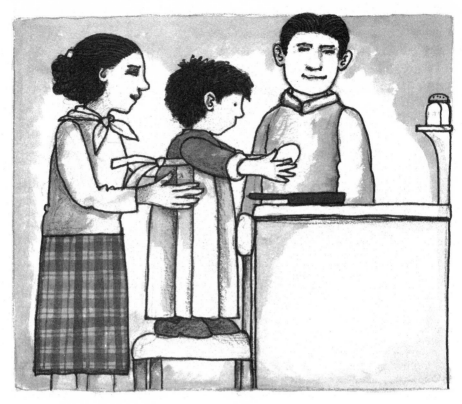

iron frying pan and put it on the stove. Then he put a chair with its back against the stove for me to stand on.

Mom turned on the stove, and I dropped some butter into the frying pan until it sizzled. Mom and Dad stood on either side of me—just in case, I guess.

I took the "hole" and fried it in the butter until it was crispy. I did the same thing with one side of the piece of bread. Then I turned

it over and carefully poured the egg into the hole. It cooked some more. I turned it over again, and it was done. I put it on a plate and put the fried "hole" on top. It was delicious!

Chapter Four

On Sunday, after mass, Dad made pancakes for my *real* birthday breakfast—pancakes and sausages—another of my favorites.

"Birthday presents when we get home from Wallingford," Mom said.

The doorbell rang. It was my best friend, Jeannie Houdlette. She had a package all wrapped up with a ribbon and a brown paper bag in her hand. "Happy birthday, Tomie," Jeannie said.

"Thanks, Jeannie!"

I unwrapped her present. It was a book of fairy tales with beautiful pictures. I looked in the paper bag. Her mother had made home-made doughnuts!

After lunch, we went to Wallingford. Mom visited with Nana. Tom read the funny papers to Buddy and me.

"How about a walk?" Tom asked when he finished the funnies. Buddy and I got our coats. We walked down North Whittlesey Avenue, past Holy Trinity School. We looked at the cutouts in all the school windows. Today there were colored leaves.

"Well," Tom said as we turned the corner. "What do you know, we're right here at O. D. Foote's Ice Cream Parlor. Let's go in."

This wasn't a real surprise because we went to Foote's every Sunday to get ice cream. Buddy would always have a hot fudge sundae. I'd have a coffee ice cream sundae with "dust" on it.

Tom always told me that the "dust" was from Mr. Foote's store. He said that because Mr. Foote made ice cream and candy there, all the dust was sweet, so Mr. Foote saved it to put on sundaes. Of course, I knew it wasn't really dust. It was malt.

But this Sunday, I wondered why we didn't sit down for sundaes. But I didn't ask. Instead, Tom bought some tubs of ice cream and some fruit slices for Nana.

"O.D.," Tom said to Mr. Foote, "today is Tomie's birthday. He's six years old."

Mr. Foote gave me a root beer–flavored lollipop. "For free," he said.

"That's the first time he *ever* gave anyone anything for free," Tom told me when we were outside.

As we walked up the block to Tom and Nana's house, there were some cars parked in front. What was going on?

We opened the door. "Surprise! Happy birthday!" The house was full of relatives and friends, all shouting and waving.

It was like a grown-up party with cake and punch and sandwiches with the crusts cut off. Aunt Nell had made celery stalks stuffed with cream cheese that had cherry juice mixed in it to make it sweet and pink.

There were presents, too. I got my own game of Chinese checkers just like the one at Tom and Nana's house, as well as a lot of other things.

"Well," Aunt Nell said, "six years old is quite an age, isn't it?"

I gave Aunt Nell a big hug.

Chapter Five

After all the excitement of my birthday celebrations, what was going to be next?

Halloween, that's what. It was only a month away.

Meanwhile, fall was on the way. The leaves were changing color and dropping from the trees. There were stories in all the children's magazines about Jack Frost coming at night and painting the leaves.

Jeannie and I found especially beautiful leaves. Mom showed us how to put the leaves between pieces of waxed paper, then place a piece of brown paper underneath and another piece on top. Next, Mom heated the electric iron and pressed it down on top of the brown paper—first one side, and then the other. The wax from the waxed paper melted onto the leaves. Now they wouldn't dry out and lose their color.

Whenever we went downtown, I looked at all the Halloween stuff in the stores. Mom always made our costumes, but I liked to figure out what I wanted to be. So far I didn't have any good ideas.

The stores had a lot of their Halloween stuff out, especially the two five- and ten-cent stores, Woolworth's and Kresge's. The candy counters had trays of candy corn and chocolate pumpkins, licorice cats and witches, and candy jack-o'-lanterns.

The toy counters were filled with masks and costumes, papier-mâché pumpkins that you could put a flashlight in, orange and black streamers, cutout witches and black cats, and long jointed skeletons to hang in doorways—all kinds of spooky, scary things.

This year I would be old enough to go out trick-or-treating with Buddy, and when it was dark, too! So I wanted just the right costume. I knew Buddy wouldn't be any help. He always wanted to be a bum. You know—clothes too big, dirty face, old hat. Mom would have some good ideas. She always did.

Then guess what happened? I found the perfect idea for a costume in Wallingford.

On Saturdays, Dad, Buddy, and I always went to Nana and Tom's grocery store to help out. This Saturday, Mom went, too.

Just as we arrived, Uncle Charles came in from helping to deliver the groceries to customers' houses.

"C'mon, boys," he said to Buddy and me. "Let's go up to Charlie's Store and get you some comic books."

Charlie sold all kinds of things—ice cream, comic books, magazines, newspapers, and because of the time of the year, lots of Halloween things. After I had picked out a couple of comic books, I started looking at the Halloween stuff. Then I saw them. Two masks. I ran all the way back to Tom and Nana's store.

"Mom, Mom," I said. "Please come with me. I found what Buddy and I could be for Halloween."

Mom came with me. I showed her the masks.

"Well, Buddy, what do you think?" Mom asked my brother, who was busy sitting on the floor, reading a Dick Tracy comic.

"I guess it's okay," he answered.

Mom bought the masks. She bought a black wig in a box and a smiling cat rattle for Maureen.

"Don't tell *anyone* what we are going to be," I told Mom on the way home. "That means you, too, Buddy."

I couldn't wait for Mom to begin our costumes. She had already made an adorable clown suit for Maureen. She sewed and sewed and sewed all week. She finally finished them on Halloween morning.

That afternoon I helped Mom make all the little packs of candy we would give out at

our house. We put different kinds of candy in orange-and-black Halloween napkins and tied them with black paper ribbon. Mom put them on a tray and put the tray on the table near the front door. Dad had carved a jack-o'-lantern and put a lit candle in it. It was sitting outside on the top step by the door.

"It's almost five-thirty!" Mom called down the stairs. Buddy and I raced upstairs to get dressed. There was Maureen in her little clown suit. She looked so cute. "Okay, boys, you're next."

Mom helped Buddy into the long black robe with the black cape and pointed hood. He put on the mask. He looked really good! Now me. I stepped into my costume. Mom zipped up the back. She helped me put on my mask and wig.

There we were!

30

Snow White and the Wicked Witch.

We looked just like the movie. No one
would know it was Buddy and I.

We'll get so much candy, I thought. I could hardly wait to start.

"Now, don't forget, all the kids are going to come here at seven-thirty for a party," Mom said. "That should give you plenty of time to go to lots of houses."

Buddy—or should I say the Wicked Witch, complete with the poisoned apple—lit his—her—flashlight. Then Mom said, "Oops, wait a minute. It's cold out. Tomie, come get a sweater."

"Snow White didn't wear a sweater. It'll ruin my costume!" I protested.

"Okay," Mom said. "You can wear it underneath the costume. But you're not going out there without it!"

There I was, Snow White—perfect—even the yellow bow in my black wig— except for the arms of my sweater sticking out of the pretty yellow puffed sleeves of my costume.

"C'mon, *Snow White*," Buddy said. "And no singing!" He had heard me practicing some of the Snow White songs from the movie. So, off we went.

"Where shall we start?" I asked Buddy.

"Let's go down Highland Avenue and work our way back up," Buddy said. He had figured it all out. His friends who had lived in the neighborhood before us had told him which houses gave out the best stuff. "Who wants apples?" Buddy said. "I'm after the CANDY!"

We ran the doorbell of the Meahs' house. Mrs. Meah opened the door. "OOOOH! Who do we have here? Why, it's Snow White and the Wicked Witch! Let's see if I can guess who you really are."

This was going to be good.

"Are you the Del Favaro children?" she asked. We shook our heads. She tried again and was wrong again.

If she couldn't guess, we'd get MORE candy. That was a "rule" in our neighborhood.

"Wait," she said. "Are you the Clark children from Prospect Avenue?"

We did it!

"NO." We shook our heads.

As she held out the candy bowl to us, she added, "I wonder if you remember the words to some of your songs, Snow White."

Buddy pinched my rear end HARD.

"I'll give you a chocolate bar if you do," Mrs. Meah said.

I sang the song about the prince coming someday, complete with gestures. Mrs. Meah clapped and gave each of us a big chocolate bar.

When we left, Buddy said, "I thought I told you, no singing!"

"I got us extra candy, didn't I?" I answered back.

Well, we were a huge success! No one knew who we were! We got tons of candy everywhere. The Wicked Witch had a big black bag. Snow White had a big basket with a checked cloth on top. They were both full in no time.

The only problem was that Buddy wanted to eat some of his candy, which was hard to do with a mask on, so by the time we got home for the party, the Wicked Witch's lips were all soggy!

Next year I'd go out by myself.

Chapter Six

All the grown-ups were talking about Thanksgiving being a week earlier than usual. Last year President Roosevelt had changed it to the third Thursday in November from the fourth Thursday. He did it to help the "economy," whatever that was. He said it gave the stores an extra week to sell things for the Christmas season, which began on Thanksgiving weekend.

Uncle Charles liked to decorate one of the windows at Tom and Nana's store. Now that I was six, I could really help him. We put real cornstalks along the wall with real pumpkins and big blue squashes among them.

Then Uncle Charles put a horn-thing that he called a "cornucopia" in the middle of everything, and we filled it full of wax fruit. Apples, oranges, grapes, and real walnuts spilled out of the opening. Next to it we put a big turkey made out of crepe paper with its tail all spread out. I thought the window looked beautiful.

The store was very busy. Nana was on the phone taking down all the orders.

"What size turkey would you like?" she asked. "Fifteen pounds? Are you sure that will be big enough? How many people will be at dinner? . . . Oh yes, that will be fine!"

Tom's walk-in refrigerator was filled with turkeys of all sizes.

"See this one?" Tom said. "This big one is for our Thanksgiving dinner." We always went to Tom and Nana's for Thanksgiving dinner—and Christmas, too.

This year I was going to make the place cards for the dining room table. Last year Uncle Charles had little painted clay turkeys with wire feet to put at everyone's place. I decided I'd draw Pilgrim men and women on the place cards next to each name— Nana, Tom, Mom, Dad, Uncle Charles, Mickey Lynch (Uncle Charles's best friend), Buddy, Maureen, and Tomie.

When we got to Wallingford and opened the door to Nana's, it smelled so good. I ran into the kitchen. Nana was at the big black stove stirring one of the pots and pans simmering on top of it.

She opened the oven door and showed me the roasting turkey.

"Wow, Nana, it's huge!" I said.

"Do you think we'll have enough?" Nana asked, smiling.

Dad helped Tom make the dining room table bigger by pulling it apart in the middle and putting in wooden pieces called "leaves."

Then Nana spread out a big white tablecloth and set the table with her best china. She let me fold the napkins and put on the place cards. I always sat next to Tom.

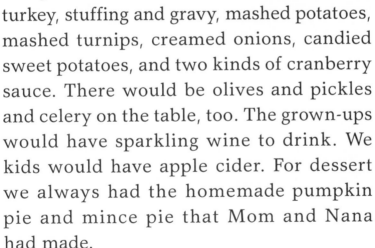

Every Thanksgiving we had the same things to eat— turkey, stuffing and gravy, mashed potatoes, mashed turnips, creamed onions, candied sweet potatoes, and two kinds of cranberry sauce. There would be olives and pickles and celery on the table, too. The grown-ups would have sparkling wine to drink. We kids would have apple cider. For dessert we always had the homemade pumpkin pie and mince pie that Mom and Nana had made.

"Okay, everyone," Nana called from the dining room.

We all went in and sat down.

Tom said grace to thank God for "all the blessings we received."

Then Nana brought in the huge golden turkey. Tom picked up the big carving knife and fork and cut the first slice off the turkey. Everyone clapped. "Who wants dark meat, who wants a wing, who wants the other leg?" Our feast began.

After dinner we were so full that Dad, Tom, Buddy, and I all dozed off in the living room. Uncle Charles and Mickey Lynch went

to see Uncle Charles's girlfriend, Viva. Mom and Nana did the dishes and talked while baby Maureen slept in her carriage.

When we woke up, Buddy, Tom, and I played Chinese checkers, and Nana packed up turkey and stuffing and gravy for us to take home so we could have hot turkey sandwiches.

It was the same every Thanksgiving. (Except Maureen got bigger and bigger and didn't sleep in her carriage anymore.)

The next day we went downtown. Mom was taking Jeannie and me to the movies. *Pinocchio*, a brand-new Walt Disney movie, was playing at the Capitol Theatre. Pinocchio is a marionette (that's a puppet with strings) made of wood that comes to life and tries to become a real boy. The movie had music and wonderful characters just like in *Snow White and the Seven Dwarfs*. My favorite part was when Pinocchio danced with marionettes from different countries. It reminded me of our dancing school recital at Miss Leah's, in a way.

When it was over, I asked Mom if I could go see it again. I sure liked Mr. Walt Disney's movies.

"We'll see," Mom said.

We went outside, and Buddy was waiting for us. He had come downtown with us, but he had been to the Palace to see a cowboy movie. I think he thought he was too old for a cartoon, even though it was long like a regular movie.

It was already dark, so we hurried to West Main Street where Santa was going to turn on the Christmas lights to start the Christmas season. Lots of people were on the streets.

Suddenly we heard sleigh bells, and all the traffic stopped. Down West Main Street came Santa Claus in a sleigh pulled by two horses. Everyone waved and whistled.

Santa called out, "Merry Christmas, everyone! Only twenty-seven shopping days left before Christmas!" It was really thirty-two days until Christmas, but Santa didn't count Sundays.

The sleigh stopped by the big traffic tower that was in the middle of where West Main Street, Colony Street, and East Main Street all came together. Santa got out and pulled a big switch on the base of the tower.

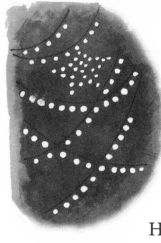

All the Christmas lights along the streets came on. Everyone *ooooh*ed and *ahhhh*ed and clapped.

We walked along to the barbershop where Dad worked. He was just finishing up.

"Hello, everyone," Dad said. "How about going for pizza?" And he took us all to Verdolini's Restaurant.

"A great way to start the Christmas season, right?" Dad asked.

"Yes!" we all shouted.

Chapter Seven

Now that it was really the "Christmas season," I started making my three Christmas lists. *List Number 1*: what I wanted to give to each person. *List Number 2*: what I wanted to get from my family. *List Number 3*: what I wanted Santa Claus to bring me.

On *List Number 1* I wrote:

A Buddy series book for my brother, Buddy

A corncob pipe for Tom

A pretty handkerchief for Nana and one for Nana Fall-River, too

A bow tie for Uncle Charles

A doll for Maureen

A paper doll book for Jeannie

Cologne for Mom (That's perfume, but it isn't as strong and it doesn't cost as much money.)

I wasn't sure what to give Dad, but Mom said she'd help me out. I wanted to get a present for Miss Kiniry, too!

I couldn't decide what *I* wanted to get! I really wanted a wood-burning set, but I knew I was too young. So I just put down on my list, "ANYTHING ANYONE WANTS TO GIVE ME!"

List Number 3 was really important. For Santa I wrote a letter:

Dear Santa Claus

Most of all, I would really like to get a Flexible Flyer sled just like the big kids have. But I would take anything else that you want to leave. My sister Maureen is too little to write a letter. I know she would like a pretty doll.

Thank you.

Tomie dePaola (at school they call me Tommy.)

P.S. This is a new address. We used to live at 53 Columbus Avenue in the downstairs apartment. Now we live at 26 Fairmount Avenue.

Please don't get lost.

We had to buy figures for the new manger scene that would go on the mantel of the real fireplace. So Mom took me downtown on a Friday night when the stores were open.

In all the stores, the counters were filled with all kinds of decorations, trees and wreaths, glass ornaments from other countries, ropes of glass beads, tinsel, boxes of foil icicles, strings of colored lights—everything you could think of. Christmas music was playing everywhere.

We looked at the manger scene figures in both Woolworth's and Kresge's. The ones at Woolworth's were bigger, so we decided we'd buy those. We bought Mary, Saint Joseph, a kneeling shepherd, a standing shepherd with a lamb around his neck, some standing sheep, and some lying down. We bought a donkey, a cow, three camels, and the three kings. We bought a new stable with a silver star on top that we could put a Christmas light in. We bought some angels and a palm tree. And, of course, a beautiful baby Jesus in a little wooden manger with real hay in it. *Our manger scene will be as beautiful as the one in the church*, I thought.

On Monday afternoon when we went back to school after lunch, Miss Kiniry passed out some little booklets. Our class was going to put on a Christmas play at the Christmas assembly. Everyone would be in it.

The main characters were two children, a boy and a girl, waiting for Santa Claus. Anyone could try out for a part. This time I was lucky. Miss Kiniry picked me to play the little boy. (Not like last year when I talked too much and didn't get to play Peter Rabbit.) She picked Jean Minor to play the little girl. Jack Rule was the tallest boy in our class, so he got to be Santa Claus. My friend Jeannie was kind of tall, too, so she would be the mother.

I couldn't wait to start "rehearsals." That's when we all practiced our parts so that we would remember our lines on the day of the performance.

Then, disaster struck.

Chapter Eight

After only three rehearsals, I woke up itchy. When I took off my pajama top, my chest had some spots on it.

"Mom!" I yelled. She came running.

"Don't scratch!" she cried, and put a thermometer in my mouth. "You have a temperature. Get back in bed. I'm going to call the doctor, and I'll be right back."

It seemed that every few minutes another itchy spot popped out. Mom came in with a cloth and a bottle of witch hazel. She sponged me off to make me not quite so itchy.

In a short while, Dr. Towers came. He examined me.

"Well, young man," Dr. Towers said. "You have chicken pox!"

"But Doctor," Mom said, "he's already had them. Remember when Buddy got them? Tomie did, too—a few days later. I thought you could only get them once."

"Well, he's got 'em again. And this time he's really got 'em."

The house was in an uproar. First, Mom and Dad moved Maureen's crib and all her things into their room. Mom made up the daybed that was in Maureen's little room. That would be my bedroom while I was sick. I'd have to be all alone because chicken pox is *very* contagious. Even though Buddy had already had it, Mom and Dad weren't taking any chances.

It seemed as though every time we looked, there were more spots. Mom gave me a bath with some stuff in it to make me less itchy. By the next day, I had chicken pox EVERYWHERE— in my hair, in my ears, up my nose, on the bottoms of my feet, in between my toes, on my behind—EVERYWHERE!!!

Dr. Towers gave Mom some medicine to make the itching feel better. I'd have to stay in bed until every single spot got a little scab on it and fell off by itself. If I scratched the scab off, I'd have little scars. So it was important for me to be good about it. It would take a while.

Meanwhile, Mom tried to make me as comfortable as possible. She cut the legs of my pajamas short so the chicken pox on my knees wouldn't itch as much. I couldn't walk because of the chicken pox on the bottoms of my feet. It was awful!

But I was worried about other things, too. I missed everyone. Mom and Dad would come in to see me. But I couldn't get near Maureen, and Buddy would just stand at the door and tell me about all the fun he was having at school.

That's another thing I was worried about—school. I was missing all the reading and other lessons. I couldn't have a reading book because I was too contagious. But Miss Kiniry sent home lessons for Mom to help me with so I wouldn't be too far behind when I got better.

Most of all, I was worried about the play. Mom helped me every day with my lines. But what if I didn't get better in time?

"Don't worry," Mom said. "Dr. Towers is pretty sure you'll be well in time to be in the play."

"What about my Christmas shopping?" I asked.

"Don't worry," Mom said again.

Everyone tried to be as nice as they could to me. Jeannie sent me a get-well card. My grandfather, Tom, made me funny pictures on the paper he wrapped the meat in at the store. Of course, Mom read me stories every night, and I was allowed to have a small radio in the room so I could hear my programs.

I listened to "Little Orphan Annie," "Tom Mix," "Jack Armstrong," and "Captain Midnight."

Of course, at noontime I listened to Cousin Morton. A new program had started on Saturday morning—"Let's Pretend." Every week a group of actors would put on a radio play based on a fairy or folk tale or a children's book. It was my favorite of all. I never missed it once it started.

I had to wait until every single spot scabbed over and fell off before I was no longer contagious. It took weeks and weeks. Finally I was able to go back to school. Some of the other kids were out sick with chicken pox, too. Miss Kiniry and the class were all glad to see me.

We rehearsed the play in the morning and again in the afternoon because the next day was the Christmas assembly! But I knew all my lines, so it wasn't a problem.

When the curtain went up the next morning, I was ready! Mom had bought me a new bathrobe, slippers, and pajamas for the play. Jean Minor wore the same thing, except she wore a nightgown instead of pajamas. It was supposed to be Christmas Eve. That's why we wore pajamas.

Everyone was so good that we got a "standing ovation." (That's when everyone stands up and claps because they liked the play so much!)

And guess what! That day we started our two weeks' Christmas vacation!

Chapter Nine

Mom took me downtown to do my Christmas shopping. While I had chicken pox, it had snowed. So downtown looked like a postcard.

It was really fun going to all the stores. When we got to Upham's Department Store, I asked Mom to leave me by myself. Even though I was only six, I knew Upham's by heart. It wasn't really that big.

I went to the perfume counter.

"Hello, little boy. Can I help you?"

I climbed up on one of the tall stools in front of the counter. "I want to get my mother a bottle of cologne for Christmas. My dad wrote down the name of the one she likes, and he gave me the money for it."

"Before you buy it, would you like to smell some others?" the lady asked. She squirted from several bottles. They all smelled good.

"Now," she said, "this is Tweed, the one your mother likes."

It smelled the best of all. I paid for it.

The lady took my money. She wrote something on a piece of paper. Then she put the money and the paper in a little metal box and clipped it on some wires that ran all around the ceiling of the store. The little box went zooming along to the "Cashier's Cage" in the back of the store. In a few minutes the box came zooming back with my change in it.

"Now, if you want it gift-wrapped, go to the counter over there," the lady said.

I got to pick out the paper and ribbon. Mom was going to love it!

The rest of the days before Christmas were very busy—putting up the tree, the manger scene, and the village, Mom making Christmas cookies, and wrapping packages. We put electric candles with blue bulbs in every window of the house. Dad hung strings of blue lights on the big bushes along the front of the house.

We were ready, and BINGO, it was Christmas Eve. Buddy, Maureen, and I had on our new pajamas, slippers, and bathrobes.

Mine were the ones I had worn in the play. Mysterious presents were piled up under the tree. We were allowed to open one each before we went to bed. I got a special bar of soap that looked like a duck.

My parents were having a party with all their friends and neighbors called an "open house."

Mom was all dressed up, and so was Dad.

"Okay," Mom said, carrying Maureen upstairs. "Everyone to bed so Santa Claus can come."

This year, I was going to stay awake so I could see him. I figured out how I could lie down by the stairs and peek so no one could see *me*, but I could see anyone coming near the stairs. This year, our first Christmas in 26 Fairmount Avenue, I would stay awake and catch Santa!

The light from the candles in the window filled the room with blue light. Buddy was fast asleep. I wasn't.

I was waiting. I was sure I'd hear the bells of Santa's sleigh and the sound of the hooves of his reindeer on the roof. As soon as I did, I'd creep to the stairs and watch.

I heard the guests coming for the open house. It sounded like everyone was having a good time.

Dad had told me that when it was almost midnight, everyone would go downstairs to the basement party room so Santa could come. That's what I was waiting for. I'd hear the grown-ups going to the basement, then I'd hear the jingle bells and I'd see HIM.

I only closed my eyes for a minute, or so I thought. I heard bells. I jumped out of bed as quietly as I could and crept to the stairs. There was one of our neighbors playing with a xylophone. It was one of our presents from Santa—I MISSED HIM—I couldn't believe it!

Well, I thought, *I might as well go downstairs.*

There were lots of people all having a good time.

"Oh, look who we have here. Merry Christmas, Tomie," Jeannie Houdlette's mother said.

"The noise woke me up," I told her.

"Look what Santa brought you," another neighbor said.

But Mom turned me around to face the stairs. "Okay, okay," she said. "Back to bed. You have to wait until morning!"

"Nice try," Dad whispered as I went up the stairs.

I tried to remember what I saw, but there was so much.

The next morning, bright and early, I was downstairs with Buddy. He got a brand-new bike. It was a Columbia, and it was bright red! There was my sled. It was a Junior Flexible Flyer, but that was okay. It would be easier to pull.

Santa had brought me so many things—a Mickey Mouse and Donald Duck train set, a children's phonograph, and some records of nursery rhymes set to music.

Under the tree was a model farm, with a house, barn, sheds, animals, and people. There were stuffed toys, a paint set, and some books.

Uncle Charles gave me a game of the World's Fair. The card said, "So you don't forget." We had all gone to the World's Fair last year.

Even though Maureen was only nine months old, she could walk. So Santa not only brought her all kinds of dolls and toys, but a doll's baby carriage. She looked so cute pushing it all around. Dad took home movies of us all.

There was one present left to open. It was a big box. "It's the Family Present," Dad said. "We'll open it when we get home from church."

St. Joseph's was all decorated with red flowers called poinsettias. Up at the front was the manger scene. It was almost life-size. The three kings weren't there. "Where are the kings?" I asked.

One of the sisters who taught Sunday school heard me and whispered, "The kings haven't gotten to Bethlehem yet. Maybe they'll get here in a few days."

I liked that idea. So when we got home, Mom moved the kings down to the end of the mantel. "We'll move them a little closer each day," Mom said.

"Let's open the Family Present," Dad said. We all gathered around as Dad opened the box. Inside was a big machine that looked like a phonograph. "It *is* a phonograph," Dad said, "but it makes records, too!"

Oh, boy, I would be able to sing all the songs I knew and play them over and over again. "Can we make one now?" I shouted.

"We'll have to wait until we get home from Wallingford and Christmas dinner," Mom said.

Nana and Tom had a little Christmas tree in the front hall. There were some small gifts under it. We added our presents to the pile.

After a delicious Christmas dinner and after Nana had brought a flaming plum pudding to the table for dessert, we opened our presents.

Tom loved his pipe and Nana said she was going to save her handkerchief for "best."

Tom gave each of us a silver dollar, and Nana gave me my very own diary. Starting on New Year's Day, I'd be able to write my private thoughts. The best thing was that the diary had a lock and key so NOBODY—read: Buddy—could sneak a peek!

Chapter Ten

"Because it's our first New Year's Eve in our new house, we're going to have a party," Dad told us.

"And Tomie, you can stay up as late as you want!" Mom said.

Oh, boy. I'd get to say "Happy New Year" to all the grown-ups at midnight.

This wasn't the first time I had stayed up until midnight, though. I "saw the New Year in" when I was only three years old.

Mom and Dad were going to a New Year's Eve dance at the Elks Club in Wallingford. They got all dressed up. They were going with Uncle Charles, his girlfriend, Viva, their friend Mickey Lynch, and Mr. and Mrs. Pickett. It was the first time Mom and Dad had been to a dance since I was born.

Buddy and I would stay at Tom and Nana's. Nana's cousin Kitty was visiting, too. Cousin Kitty was the mother of my twin cousins who were studying to be artists in New York.

"Be a good boy," Mom told me when we got to Tom and Nana's house. "I'll pick you up later." Mom didn't tell me then, but "later" meant the next morning.

Well, as it got later, Tom and Buddy went to bed. "It's time for you to go to sleep," Nana said.

"I'm waiting for Mommy," I said. "She said she'd pick me up." I guess Mom thought I'd get tired and go to sleep. But I didn't.

I just sat there in Nana's parlor— waiting.

Nana fell asleep in her chair. Cousin Kitty fell asleep in hers.

On the way home, Mom and Dad had to drive by Nana and Tom's. The front porch light was on even though it was three o'clock in the morning, so they stopped and parked.

It's a good thing they did, because when they walked in, there I was sitting up in a chair, wide-awake. Nana and Cousin Kitty were sound asleep.

They woke up when they heard Mom and Dad come in. "See," I said, "I told you Mommy was going to pick me up!"

This was a different New Year's Eve.

I was six. I had my very own diary with the key on a string around my neck. I took it off, put it in the lock, and opened it up.

At last it was time to start writing in my diary. I made a list of everything exciting that had happened this past year—1940.

December 31, 1940 NEW YEAR'S EVE

Dear Diary,

Here are some important things that happened this year.

Moving into the new house

My baby sister Maureen is born

Maureen going to the hospital, but getting better

Dancing in Miss Leah's recital

Having Miss Kiniry as my first grade teacher

Learning to read

Getting my library card

My birthday party at school

My first Halloween in our new neighborhood

Chicken pox – UGH!

Sledding on my Junior Flexible Flyer from Santa

Staying up on New Year's Eve– TO-NIGHT!!!!!

GOOD-BYE, SEE YOU LATER,

Tomie

I finished writing just as the guests started to arrive for our party. I ran to Aunt Nell to show her what I had written in my diary.

"Oh, Tomie," she said. "What a year!"

The End

(I wonder what 1941 will be like?)

Tomie dePaola is known for his popular picture books about his childhood, including *Nana Upstairs & Nana Downstairs* and *The Baby Sister*. He is the recipient of a Caldecott Honor award and the Regina Medal. *26 Fairmount Avenue,* his first chapter book and the first book in this series, is a Newbery Honor Book.